Be Resilient

Book One:
Free Your Glorious Self

Patricia Thatcher

Copyright © 2014 Patricia Thatcher. All rights reserved. No portion of this book may be reproduced mechanically, electronically, or by any other means, including photocopying, without written permission of the publisher. It is illegal to copy this book, post it to a website, or distribute it by any other means without permission from the publisher.

Patricia Thatcher
The LifeWorks Center
2464 Massachusetts Avenue, Suite 312, Cambridge, Ma 02140
617-661-1277 patthatch@thelifeworkscenter.com
www.thelifeworkscenter.com

Limits of Liability and Disclaimer of Warranty

The author and publisher shall not be liable for your misuse of this material. This book is strictly for informational and educational purposes.

Warning – Disclaimer

The purpose of this book is to educate and is not intended to replace professional psychotherapy. The author and/or publisher do not guarantee that anyone following these techniques, suggestions, tips, ideas, or strategies will become successful. The author and/or publisher shall have neither liability nor responsibility to anyone with respect to any loss or damage caused, or alleged to be caused, directly or indirectly by the information contained in this book.

Get Inspired Everyday!
Qualities with Inspirational Quotes for Your Glorious Self

Here is a bonus especially for you.

These inspirational quotes will help you in your quest to connect more fully with Your Glorious Self.

With this free download you can:
- Pick a Quality a Day
- Read the inspirational quotes
- Connect with the message
- Bring it fully into your being
- Live life to the fullest

Go Here: **http://bit.ly/1qyNNMd** to download your very own copy of **Qualities with Inspirational Quotes for Your Glorious Self**

It's absolutely FREE!

Website: www.thelifeworkscenter.com

Acknowledgements

It truly takes a village to complete a project, even one as small as this. I would not be where I am today without some wonderful mentors, friends and supporters. My journey has been exciting and challenging. Every experience has helped me along the way to become a seasoned psychotherapist who has the privilege of helping others. While I am sometimes the guide, I am always guided by the client and learn as much from them as they do from me.

First I would like to thank all the clients who shared their pain and sorrow with the hope that I could help them. Together we forged new territory so they could process that pain and hurt in order to create more happiness.

Training in Ericksonian Hypnosis led the way to me being open to several new, innovative ways to help folks clear the ravaging effects of early traumatic experience. This included the meridian therapies, especially Tapas Acupressure Technique® (TAT®) and EMDR (Eye Movement Desensitization and Reprocessing). Since I learned both modalities around the same time in 1996 they became intricately entwined in my work with trauma survivors.

I am deeply indebted to Tapas Fleming for her willingness to share her knowledge, experience and love of life with me as I sought to find ways to bring

TAT into my work and life. By 1998 I knew I wanted to share this amazing modality more formally with colleagues. Tapas and I worked together for a year in preparation for me to teach others and bring TAT more and more into the world. It is now used internationally on every continent. One of my favorite photos is of a group of people in tsunami-torn Indonesia holding the TAT pose as they practice disaster preparedness.

Be Resilient: Free Your Glorious Self

I would also like to thank Dr. Deborah Korn who is a magnificent coach and trainer in EMDR. Dr. Korn has an intricate understanding of how trauma affects one's life especially early developmental trauma. She is also an outstanding teacher whom I use as a model for presenting difficult and complex material. It was from Dr. Korn that I fully recognized the importance of resource development to aid everyone dealing with adverse life events.

I am grateful to all the many folks who assisted me in bringing this document into the world. Several years ago I created three short workshops to help participants develop and strengthen positive resources enough so they could do what they needed to lead more fulfilling and satisfying lives. This manuscript is reflective of the first workshop: Be Resourced: Developing Positive Qualities of Self.

Thank you to Donna Kozik and Write a Book in a Weekend for providing the direction for me to buckle down and do the work of writing. Thanks to all the readers who have given me their feedback especially Beth Rontal, book buddy Betty-Anne Howard, editor Vincenza Parelli, and all the professional colleagues who offered me their support and encouragement along the way. A special thanks to Martha O'Neil, an outstanding technical advisor and computer wizard who helped me get this manuscript into book form. And, John Friendsmith, for his computer expertise through the years.

I am deeply grateful for the loving support and excellent advice of my husband, Simon Volpini.

DEDICATION

This is dedicated to every client, family member, teacher, colleague and friend who shared their lives with me while we walked side by side sharing our journeys.

Forward by Tapas Fleming

You know you're watching someone who's mastered something because they make it look so easy. It seems effortless and you might even wonder, "could it really be that simple?"

Pat Thatcher has mastered helping us connect with our inner resources and given us a way to access her knowledge in this book.

Pat is the first person who asked me if she could teach TAT® (Tapas Acupressure Technique) because she thought it was so effective with her clients and for herself, too. We took our time and she became the first TAT Trainer. That was back in 1999. Pat's been teaching TAT® since then, using it with clients and keeping up on the latest changes for all these years.

She's deeply dedicated to her own growth (not all therapists are!) and the growth of the people she helps. She walks her talk. I always feel like she's going to keep walking till she gets to her goal, no matter what it takes.

Her clients are lucky to work with her in sessions and we're lucky to have her sharing her knowledge and years of experience through this book.

This book not only teaches you how to immediately access inner resources you might not have even known you had, you actually feel uplifted and more in touch with what's possible for you just from reading the book! The exercises Pat gives are simple, powerful and effective. I know -- I tried one out and it worked for me!

Tapas Fleming, Creator of Tapas Acupressure Technique®

Be Resilient: Free Your Glorious Self

Contents

Chapter 1: Welcome 9

Chapter 2: Become Acquainted with Your Resources 21

Chapter 3: Identify the Problem 33

Chapter 4: Clear any Blocks Preventing You From Fully Embodying These Resources 49

Chapter 5: Fully Integrate These Qualities Into Your Life 79

Chapter 6: Qualities and Characteristics 85

Chapter 7: References 91

Chapter 1: Welcome

"Beneath the busyness of our daily lives flows a deep river of creativity, passion, silence and a place of contact with ourselves" Abby Seixas

Dear Reader,

Deep inside you is a Glorious Being that just needs a little help to be released. No matter how hurt you are, how sad and alone you feel, how damaged your life appears, or how miserable you may be, there is hope for a better way.

This workbook is designed to assist you in strengthening your internal resources, develop positive qualities of your Self, and build connections to external resources. The purpose is to help you feel good about yourself, most of the time, and create the life you want.

A resource is anything that will support you. Internal resources help you to deal with challenges in productive ways. If you are going for a job interview you want to connect with the qualities of competence and confidence. If you are going to a party you want to be happy and have fun.

External resources provide support from the environment. These are supportive people like parents and friends. So too is your job, home and the food you eat. Anything that is outside of yourself, that supports your living a happy, healthy life, is an external resource.

Sometimes making a small change can quickly connect you with all the resources you need. For example, if you're going to a party and you're worried about your outfit the worry can keep you from being really happy and having fun. Maybe all you have to do is change your outfit or just change your attitude about the outfit to be more in the party mood.

At other times, there is more like a wall in the way and a little more work is needed to bring that wall down. Maybe you're too nervous to be fully confident in your competence when you think about the job interview. You find yourself ruminating over and over about all the ways you think you are incompetent. This workbook will address what you can do to help ease that nervousness and connect more fully with the qualities that will support you.

There may be a time when your goal is to do a deeper piece of trauma work that requires you to tolerate difficult feelings, emotions and thoughts. Unresolved trauma disconnects us from our strengths and resources. A professional guide such as a therapist can be an external resource to support your journey. This workbook will support your therapeutic process by providing a means to develop and strengthen your internal qualities of Self. This will enable you to better tolerate those difficult feelings, emotions and thoughts while you process the traumatic stress.

Your body/mind system is remarkable and capable of great change. When you focus new neural pathways develop, leading to positive beliefs and ways of being.

Having an Open Mind

"A great life starts with an open mind"
  Cheryl Richardson

Almost everyone arrives into adulthood with some adverse effects from painful experiences. This could be fighting with siblings or friends, being shamed by a teacher in front of the class, or losing a valuable possession. It may even be serious abuse or trauma that has some long-lasting negative side effects.

You have been hurt and unless you process that hurt effectively your system will find ways to avoid that pain only to find out that the avoidance is just as bad, if not worse, than the original hurt. This avoidance may appear as some form of addiction, like alcohol, gambling, or problems with eating (overeating or under eating). Maybe it is relationship difficulties, work or physical/medical problems. Maybe you have anxieties and phobias.

Even though you are diligent in finding ways to avoid the pain, it inevitably surfaces. You are destined to relive over and over again that which you seek to avoid. Those parts of you that are disconnected will keep coming back to the pain and the hurt until you take stock, face it, process it, and move forward. In order to do this you have to connect with enough resources to help you complete the process.

Developing Positive Characteristics

"In our natural state, we are glorious beings"
Marianne Williamson

With the help of parents and other adults, children develop positive characteristics that enable them to grow into secure, resilient adults. As a kid, it's easy to get overwhelmed. Everyone is bigger, they know more and the world is frequently a scary place.

Physiologically the body is hard-wired to respond to perceptions of danger i.e. that scary place. It does this by disconnecting the upper front part of the brain, whose job it is to make sense of the world with the lower internal part of the brain that controls emotions. When this happens it's easy to get overwhelmed with emotions that are hard to handle, like fear, sadness and anger.

With the help of compassionate, empathetic, and understanding adults, a child learns to feel, then release the emotions and reconnect to the part of the brain that is capable of making sense of the experience. They find new meaning in their lives. The brain is building the networks for this meaning. The child develops positive qualities like compassion, understanding and empathy that are useful when they meet challenges in the future. This learning that happens in childhood stays with them into adulthood.

Once there was an eight year old who really loved to play ball. She enjoyed every sport with a ball including basketball, soccer, softball, and little league baseball. During every season she was sure to be on one of the teams. Whenever she had free time she would be shooting basketball hoops on the street with her friends.

One day her brother got a new baseball and she really wanted to play with it. She knew it was wrong to go into his room without permission but the longing was too great to resist.

When she could no longer endure the temptation she went into his room and began to play with the ball. The feel of it was so nice, the weight was just perfect and the desire to throw it grew and grew. She imagined pulling her arm back, reaching around and bringing it forward. Suddenly, she let go of the ball and it went flying through the window, falling in the mud outside. She felt terrible and scared. She did not mean to disrespect her brother's property. She just wanted to play with the ball.

Her brother was mad and their parents intervened. Together, they all talked things through. Her parents listened respectfully to both siblings and made some suggestions to help mend the harm done. She apologized to her brother and made amends. Her brother calmed down and everything seemed to be ok.

She still didn't feel good about herself. She was ashamed of her behavior and did not know how to ask for help to resolve it. Later, she seemed to lose interest in playing ball. When it came time to try out for the team she just didn't want to and avoided playing any kind of ball, even basketball with the kids in the neighborhood.

Her parents noticed that she was no longer interested in something she used to love. They tried to talk to her about it but she was afraid and only wanted to be left alone. There were times when she became angry. Other times she became very quiet, spending lots of time alone.

Being compassionate, her parents encouraged her to share her feelings with them. With their help, she had opportunities to re-tell the story of what happened many times in different ways. She connected to the emotions of shame, sadness, and fear. She cried and shook when she needed to.

In this safe environment she also learned some new things about herself, including that it was natural to want to avoid the difficult feelings. When she let herself feel and express the emotions, with support from her parents, she felt relief.

Her parents displayed the qualities of compassion, persistence, understanding, and empathy. This enabled her to not only heal from that experience but gave her a blueprint of how to be with herself and

Be Resilient: Free Your Glorious Self

others when difficulties arose. Mirroring their compassion she was able to forgive herself.

After a while, she was even able to connect with her love of playing ball. She found herself wanting to play basketball with her friends in the street and the desire to be on the teams came back.

It's not always like this though. What if the parents had a rough day and were not as patient and compassionate as they needed to be? Perhaps, they were not perceptive enough to recognize that the eight year old needed support. They were unable to help her process all those difficult feelings like shame and fear.

Maybe you experienced this yourself with your own parents. During times when you needed patience and compassion they reacted with indifference, yelling, or even something worse. So you had to find a way to put it away. Perhaps you deeply buried it and built defenses against the memory of it.

However, the difficult feelings persisted and had a way of coming up.

Maybe you stayed away from your version of "playing ball" after that. Maybe you went back but acted out with lots of anger or underachieved and didn't play up to your ability. Maybe you were driven to excel, not because you loved it but because there was some underlying motivation that you had to make up for something. You had to prove yourself. When a difficult experience is not fully processed the negative side effects keep coming back to haunt you even in a disguised form.

You Are An Amazing Being

"Our deepest fear is not that we are inadequate. Our deepest fear is that we are powerful beyond measure. It is our Light, not our Darkness, that most frightens us" Marianne Williamson

You are an amazing being with the capacity to fully heal and live a happy, productive life. Whether it is a momentary self-esteem crash or a longer more intense healing process, you may need some help. Certainly the hurt child within will need the help of your more wise adult Self to process the experience, learn from it, put it behind you, and move forward pulling up those learnings when you need them. You can only do this if you are connected to enough resources that enable you to tolerate what comes up as you do the healing work.

Be Resilient: Free Your Glorious Self

By applying the exercises in this workbook you can build and connect with those resources you need to face and process that hurt. When fully integrated you become more fully you, more alive, happy, loving, peaceful, resilient and on and on for you are infinite in your resourcefulness.

Marianne Williamson is right when she tells us that *"in our natural state, we are glorious beings."* It is just that as we grow and experience hurt and pain we build defenses to protect this Glorious Being within. Eventually we have hidden it even from ourselves.

Well, congratulations, you are about to become more fully acquainted with and connected to your Glorious Being!

This process is made up of five parts:
1. Identify the problem.
2. Identify the qualities you would like to help you with this problem.
3. Complete the visualization/imagery process to more fully embody these qualities.
4. Clear any blocks preventing you from embodying these qualities. (Several modalities are described including Tapas Acupressure Technique®, Breathing and visualization processes)
5. Fully integrate these qualities into your life.

Things that will be helpful as you follow this process:

- a journal or a blank notebook if you do not want to use this workbook in order to record your process
- water to drink and stay hydrated
- access to the internet so you can download important information
- a quiet place where you can be fully present with your Self
- paper, crayons, art supplies
- Post-it™ notes or something similar

"Each of us is a perfect, whole, eternal beyond time, beyond existence and unchanging embodiment of love and peace" Tapas Fleming

Be Resilient: Free Your Glorious Self

GLORIOUS BEING WITHIN

WISE SELF

- Accepting
- Present
- Compassionate
- Safe
- Connected
- Loving
- Clear
- Understanding

CHILD
- Curious
- Playful

Graphic by Beth Rontal, LICSW

Chapter 2: Become Acquainted with Your Resources

"Start by doing what's necessary; then do what's possible; and suddenly you are doing the impossible" St. Francis of Assisi

A resource is anything that will support you and/or help you to feel good about yourself and/or deal with a problem in a productive way.

Resources are:

1. Positive characteristics and qualities such as courage, strength, humor, confidence, competence, safety, etc. that either you hold within you or admire in someone else that you want to develop more strongly in yourself.
2. Positive memories that build the foundation for living a happy and healthy life.
3. A thing or an object such as a rock, nature, trees, flowers, gardens, bells, color, light, music and sounds that you spend time with or connect to.
4. A person, a spiritual being, an animal companion that you want to have with you.
5. Positive beliefs and goals.
6. Water: Any little stress dehydrates the body. Many systems do not function well when you are dehydrated. Please drink plenty of water.

Coming From a Strength Based Perspective:

"Strength does not come from physical capacity. It comes from an indomitable will" Mohandas Gandhi

The mind is a powerful playground. Engaging the imagination is useful on many levels. Recent research tells us that by focusing the mind, the brain develops new neural networks. These are pathways that create new maps for attitude and behavioral changes.

Hebb's axiom states that "Neurons that fire together wire together." When you stimulate the nervous system enough it will grow and develop new neurons that then sprout new branches (neural networks) that communicate with each other.

People who have suffered strokes can learn to move the arm or leg that has been affected because it is not their limb that is damaged but the part of the brain that controls the movement. With help, they spend hours a day slowly rebuilding new neural networks that replace the ones injured.

You can do the same to clear your trauma and build a better life. Whatever you visualize, imagine and tell yourself, your body system responds as if it is true. Stroke patients spend hours retraining their brain to build new neurons which control the movement of the limb. Eventually, when enough neurons have been connected they begin to get movement. This movement stimulates more neural networks that produce more and more movement. Small incremental steps are best in the beginning.

If a person can regrow enough neurons to move an immobile limb it is certainly possible to grow enough neurons to develop positive beliefs and behaviors. This growth usually doesn't happen on its own. It takes perseverance and a desire to do what is necessary to make those changes.

You Have Incredible Power

"The consciousness of human beings has incredible powers, to heal ourselves, to heal the world, in a sense to make it as we wish it to be"
Lynne McTaggart

Neurologists tell us that our brains work best when we are riding the tops of the hills. When the habits of living and thinking take over we find ourselves in the ruts, in the gullies. If you are giving yourself positive, happy thoughts and images, your system responds by sending those feel good chemicals throughout the body. The opposite is also true.

"When we become identified with a point of view, or something that we are not, then we can be identified with pain" Tapas Fleming

If you continually give yourself negative messages then those are the neurons that get formed. You find yourself going down the road of self-doubt and end up in the rut of self-loathing. You become identified with the negative message. You become it and it becomes you. The stress this produces prompts the body to secrete stress hormones and corticosteroids that cause damage to the nerve endings and other cells in the body.

The more you stay in that rut the more reinforced it becomes. Without thinking, your system just naturally goes there. The self-doubt and self-loathing become your normal way of being.

Remember "neurons that fire together stay together; Neurons that fire apart stay apart."

If you primarily give yourself negative messages the neurons connected to positive thoughts, beliefs, emotions, and behaviors lose connection to each other. Whole neural networks can close down.

Ralph's Story: Ralph grew up in a violent household. As an adult he experienced an intense flashback. One day his boss began to yell about something. Ralph no longer saw his boss but his father standing in front of him yelling at him.

Ralph had an immediate stress response and found himself repeating his father's words over and over. "You're bad, you're worthless, you're no good, if you don't stop crying I will give you something to cry about." He found himself responding with "I'm not safe, I won't survive this, I have to protect my family, I can't protect my family, I deserve this."

In his adult mind he knew these thoughts were not true but he could not stop them. He lost connection to his Wise Adult Self and his Glorious Being within. Soon he began to have difficulty sleeping at night, could not go out with friends and continually worried he was making mistakes at work. The more he worried the worse he got.

One day he sought outside help. Utilizing many of the modalities discussed in this manual, Ralph was able to interrupt these patterns, clear the stress and begin to give himself more positive messages. He started to sleep at night, eat more nutritiously, re-build social connections and develop the life he wanted and deserved.

The Body's Response

It is not unusual for people who are stressed to get physically sick. When stress hormones are released, the cells of the body shut down and go into defense mode. The receptors on the outside of the cell wall close ranks, reducing the nutrient intake into the cell and prevent the toxins from escaping. This is why a stressed body is more prone to illness. High levels of stress hormones can lead to a number of medical conditions including cardiovascular disease, GI diseases, adrenal fatigue, colitis, irritable bowel, high blood pressure and more.

Pat's Story: When I was pregnant I had an upsetting encounter with a friend. Within a couple of days of this upset I had a medical appointment and my blood pressure was extremely high. Usually it is on the low side. The doctor asked if I had any unusual stresses that week. Yep, that upset with my friend was the direct link to the surge in blood pressure. Consistent relaxation exercises, some extra exercise in the form of swimming and resolving the issue with my friend all helped to return my blood pressure to its usual 110/70. Had the stress responses continued I could have had serious complications.

The Triumph Begins With You

"It doesn't matter who you are, where you come from. The ability to triumph begins with you, always" Oprah Winfrey

In reality, all it takes is a little change. Let's say you go down that road of "I'm no good, I can't do anything." You notice it, you become aware of the belief and all the difficult emotions like shame, hurt, fear, and sadness that come up for you. Like Ralph, you decide "No, I am not going to cross that bridge into the land of shame." You turn yourself around and take a different road, a new road.

In the process of taking that new road you begin to develop new possibilities. You put your attention on something different, like "I am wonderful, it is ok to be happy, I can do this."

The more you tell yourself that, the more you see yourself succeeding. The more you see yourself succeeding the more you connect with the people who support you in this new way of thinking. The more you put your attention on the people who support you and those positive messages the more your brain builds those neurons. Soon whole new neural networks develop that create a happier, more satisfied you.

The Importance of Being Present

"The most precious gift we can offer others [and ourselves] is our presence" Thich Nhat Hanh

Mary Ann's Story: One day a client of mine came in and described a remarkable experience. She had been feeling negative about herself, caught in memories of awful things that happened to her as a child. She was feeling ashamed and depressed.

But this day she decided to pull out her resources. She said "I decided to think about what qualities I really needed to help me with this. I connected with those and had a conversation with my Wise Adult Self to help me more fully connect with those qualities.

I did some TAT® (Tapas Acupressure Technique®) on all the bad feelings and memories I was having. I thought about what was really good in my life now. I have a new apartment, great friends, a wonderful church community, and a good, if sometimes stressful part time job that keeps me challenged. Eventually, as I thought about all of these good things in my life I began to feel better about myself, I was able to get out of bed and move into the day in a more productive way."

Later she sent me this email "I used all my resources, consciously calling on them in another challenging moment when my adult son became angry with me. Connecting with 'my resources' I could listen to his angry words, consider them, and dialogue with him. Being resourced helped me continue a newly re-established relationship in a nurturing way rather than out of hurt and anger."

The Power of Forgiveness

"There's a physiology of forgiveness... When you do not forgive, it will chew you up" Dr. Herbert Benson

Forgiveness promotes such positive states of mind as hope, patience and self-confidence by reducing anger, suffering, depression, and stress. All the available research shows that anger, resentment and hostility seriously damages human health. The risk of heart disease is up to five times greater. Blood pressure increases and stays increased across time as long as we hold the resentment. Increases in inflammatory proteins may lead to the hardening of the arteries, causing heart disease and stroke.

Forgiveness, on the other hand, even if it is difficult, eliminates all the harmful effects of anger, and helps the individual to enjoy a healthy life. A number of studies including those conducted at Stanford University, Duke University, Johns Hopkins, and by Dr. Herbert Benson at Harvard University found that forgiveness lowers blood pressure, decreases stress reactions, reduces back ache, insomnia and stomach aches while increasing hope, patience, self-confidence and improved immunity.

Forgiveness gives back the power that was taken at the time of the hurt. But it appears to do more than that – it gives a new power, a transformed one. It does not condone the offense. It rises above it to triumph and find a new way to be with the past. Forgiveness is a way to reconnect to one's divinity and humanness with compassion, empathy and sympathy.

"Holding on to anger, resentment and hurt only gives you tense muscles, a headache and a sore jaw from clenching your teeth. Forgiveness gives you back the laughter and the lightness in your life" Joan Lunden

You Too Can Develop Resilience

"Human beings have enormous resilience"
  Muhammad Yunus

Resilience is the ability to quickly spring back and recover from difficulties or setbacks. Sometimes when people have not been able to process and get support for adverse life events in childhood their ability to be resilient is compromised. They do not seem to be able to rely on and seek out positive resources including positive qualities of Self to help them through life's challenges.

Resilience develops with:

- Positive connection to supportive and competent adults (family and community).
- Having cognitive and self-regulating abilities.
- Positive beliefs about self.
- Motivation to act effectively.

"When we tackle obstacles, we find hidden reserves of courage and resilience we did not know we had. And it is only when we are faced with failure do we realize that these resources were always there within us. We only need to find them and move on with our lives"
A. P. J. Abdul Kalam

So get prepared to build in and strengthen your resilience. Develop those positive qualities that will help you get better acquainted with and free your Glorious Being!

Chapter 3: Identify the Problem

"The goal of Resource Development is to access existing resources and develop new and effective coping skills"
Deborah Korn

- Have your journal/ notebook available or use this worksheet.
- Sit down quietly and put your attention on yourself. What is disturbing you right now, in this moment? Write this down:

_____

_____

_____

_____

_____

_____

Be Resilient: Free Your Glorious Self

- Notice your thoughts, sensations, emotions, and anything else that comes to your attention. Write these down:

Then: Identify the qualities/characteristics you would like to have to help you with this problem.

- If you can't think of two or three then check out the list of qualities in the appendix. Quickly scan and pull out two or three qualities that you are drawn to. Write these down:

_____

_____

_____

_____

_____

_____

_____

_____

Choose one quality to begin with. Describe or define this quality for yourself. Use the dictionary definition if it is helpful but the most important thing is for you to know what it means for you. Write this down:

_____

_____

_____

_____

_____

_____

_____

_____

_____

_____

_____

Learning through Observation

"A new type of neuron--called a mirror neuron--could help explain how we learn through mimicry and why we empathize with others. Mirror neurons are a type of brain cell that respond equally when we perform an action and when we witness someone else perform the same action" Lea Winerman, American Psychological Association

To fully embody these resources, do the following visualization and/or imagery process. Studies have shown that imagining something is as powerful as doing it. Even though this is called a visualization process some people do not visualize. They have thoughts, hear messages, have sensations or just an experience of knowing. However you are able to put your attention on the direction will be fine. It is helpful here to read the direction then close your eyes and put your attention on it.

When you are ready, open your eyes and write about your experience. If you would rather draw it then pull out your art materials and create it. You can do both, write and draw. Using both language and drawings stimulates the whole brain so it will benefit your whole system if you do both.

Be Resilient: Free Your Glorious Self

Direction:

Put your attention on someone you admire who has this quality or remember a time when you witnessed someone expressing this quality and/or experienced them expressing this quality towards you. Write about them here:

_____

_____

_____

_____

_____

_____

_____

_____

_____

Be Resilient: Free Your Glorious Self

Draw them here: Creativity activates a different part of the brain than language. Using your whole brain may help you get the most out of this experience. Feel free to draw if you want to, but you do not have to. Please put self-criticism aside. It does not matter what the drawing looks like. It only matters that you experience the process in a way that enriches you.

Next: bring your attention to this person, visualize them if you can or just notice all you can about them and answer the following questions. Make it up if you have to.

What do they look like as they embody this resource? What is their physical stance, how do they hold their body, what kind of expression is on their face?

_____

_____

_____

_____

_____

_____

_____

_____

_____

What kinds of things do they say?

_____

_____

_____

_____

_____

_____

How do they behave? What actions do they take?

_____

_____

_____

_____

_____

_____

What do you learn from them about this quality?

Then: Remember a time when you experienced this quality. Visualize it... Hear it... Feel it... Smell it... Taste it...

What is your experience as you fully embody this quality?

What do you look like?

_____

_____

_____

_____

_____

_____

_____

_____

Be Resilient: Free Your Glorious Self

Draw yourself here:

Be Resilient: Free Your Glorious Self

How do you feel?

What do you say?

How do you behave?
_____
_____
_____
_____
_____

Then: Cross your hands over your heart; put your attention on all you have written, visualized, felt, smelled, tasted and told yourself. Give yourself the following message. (You can read this out loud or silently.) If you read it out loud you will hear it as well as think it, which can reinforce the message.

> **This is possible for me...and is happening now...I like this...I love this...This feels wonderful... I see and hear and feel myself living this now...and taking the actions I need in order to achieve this...All of Life and all of me supports me in this...I completely allow and accept this...I am grateful for this...I choose this.**
> (Taken from workshop handout guide for Self TAT www.tatlife.com)

Practice, Practice, Practice

"Practice Makes Progress" David Roth, Musician

According to Barbara Seels, an instructional design expert, practice is the key ingredient in the learning process. When you practice you learn faster, retain it longer and remember more.

Direction:

Pick a quality a day or a quality a week. Stay present with that quality, notice it in other people, learn about it as you observe others expressing that quality or having the lack of that quality. Notice how you resonate with it and experience it. Use the directions in this workbook to fully learn about and integrate that quality. Notice what blocks are keeping you from being more fully connected to these qualities.

"An ounce of practice is worth more than tons of preaching" Mahatma Gandhi

Chapter 4: Clear any Blocks Preventing You From Fully Embodying These Resources

"One of my teachers once said that the way you know you're on the right path is that it works. Now, that doesn't mean you don't run into blocks and brick walls, but it does mean that you can find a way around them or find a way to change yourself or your project in order to find the flow again and have it work"
James Redfield

Blocks are anything that stop you from connecting to and fully utilizing your resources to live your life the way you want. Blocks prevent you from thinking, feeling and behaving from the center of your Glorious Self.

Blocks can be:

- negative beliefs about yourself and the world
- physical reactions like phobias or avoidance
- addictions like eating, smoking, drugs/alcohol, sex
- compulsions that come flying in to "Save the Day"

How would a block present itself?

Some part of you says or believes: "No way, I'm not going to let you do this, you don't deserve this, it isn't safe to feel this good, you'll just get hurt in the process."

These are stopper thoughts or limiting beliefs that come up from deep and sometimes not so deep places within your subconscious. They drive your thoughts, emotions and behaviors. They develop in response to adverse life events when you feel all alone and have to find a way to survive on your own. You do the best you can with the limited resources you have available.

It happens something like this:

You are hard wired to process experience through your senses. You talk about it, you dream about it, you may write or draw about it, you experience the emotions about it and you move with it. This movement becomes very important because you are hard wired to run and/or fight when you get stressed. This movement is what metabolizes the stress hormones and helps you to better connect with all parts of the experience.

When any part of that process is blocked or you are unable to fully process it in a way that is adaptive you are left with aspects of it hanging around as if it is still happening. It is in your face and you are responding to it as if it is still occurring. Those stress hormones go flowing through your body playing havoc with the nervous system.

Your cells go into defense mode and are less available to take in the nutrients they need from the blood flow. The immune system is less able to remove toxins. Your body becomes more open to illness and infection.

In the brain, the prefrontal cortex (the place that helps you to make sense of your experience) loses connection with the amygdala and limbic region (which is the part that controls the emotions and the fight/flight response). If all of your experience with this adversity does not integrate then pieces of the experience are disconnected. Those pieces have a way of popping in, at random, whenever anything reminds you of it. They take on a life of their own.

Be Resilient: Free Your Glorious Self

Here is an example to illustrate the fight/flight response:

A number of years ago I was hiking in the Canadian Rockies to the Patricia Lakes. I was drawn to these lakes because they were my namesake and I had a good feeling about them. I found a lovely spot to go for a swim, ate my lunch and then decided to take a short nap.

As I was just below consciousness, half in/half out of sleep, I heard some noise and thought "oh, someone is coming, I should get up." I then heard some sniffing and thought "oh, people with a dog! I really should get up."

I opened my eyes. There before me, almost touching its nose to mine, was a big black bear! I just blinked and so did the bear. It jumped back and we stared at each other for what seemed like an eternity.

I could not figure out what to do. I was frozen with no real thoughts or emotions. It seemed like forever. I slowly got up, moved backwards towards the lake, still staring at the bear, thinking "well, I'll jump in the lake if it attacks me."

I had no connection to any emotions or anything other than what I could do if it attacked. Little did I know that I could not out swim, out run or out climb a bear. The best I could do would be to stare it down and if it attacked, curl up in a ball. I did not know any of that at the time. Luckily, I did the right thing.

For a while we stared at each other, me at the edge of the water and it by the bushes. Then it just turned around and left.

I was so disconnected from my emotions that I went back to the blanket and laid down. I closed my eyes thinking I could go right back to the peaceful place I was before the bear appeared. However, in my mind's eye, I saw a big headline in the Boston Globe newspaper: **"Woman Mauled by Bear in Canadian Rockies."**

I jumped right up, quickly gathered my things and left. As I swiftly walked through the park I saw this bear a few more times getting into picnic trash cans. I did not quite believe what had happened and didn't think anyone would believe me. I was sort of in shock but I was not hurt.

As I walked down the trail into the campground I met a man who also was coming in from his adventures of the day. I told him my experience but in my heart I didn't think he would believe me. At the time I did not know why I didn't think I would be believed. I have since learned that it is common to think we will not be believed when we experience a shock or an adverse life event.

To my surprise, he not only believed me but went around telling many people in the campground about my experience. Later that night, many folks gathered around the communal campfire, sharing their stories and adventures. I got to tell my "bear" story and listen to many others. I still was not connected to any emotions, other than a kind of dull shock, even when some pretty gruesome bear stories were told.

The next morning I went hiking again, this time up a mountain. As I was walking down the road going to the trailhead I saw a bear in front of me crossing the road. I was still disconnected from emotions and was clapping two rocks together making noise to keep the bears away, a technique I learned the previous night around the campfire.

I got to the trailhead and began hiking up the hill, continuing to clap the rocks together, hoping this would be enough to keep any bears away. About half way up, all of a sudden I was frightened! I don't know why, but I fully connected to the feeling of terror in a way I never experienced before.

Without thinking, I immediately turned around and ran down that hill as fast as I could, fully embracing the flight instinct. I only remember the feeling of terror as I ran. When I got to the bottom, however, the fright was gone. I was ok. I met some folks going up to a gondola that went up to the mountain summit and joined them for the ride. All was well.

What happened to make this terror leave? When I acted on the flight response by running down that mountain the stress hormones metabolized and the terror disappeared. I moved on and have had many encounters with bears since with no adverse effects. And, now, I get to tell this great story of meeting a bear in the woods!

A maladaptive processing of a frightening experience:

About ten years later I had another exciting adverse life event, but this one did not end up with such a good outcome for me.

I was helping a client who had a phobia of driving on highways and across bridges. Back then hypnosis, imagery and desensitization were the treatments of choice for these kinds of phobic reactions. We had used imagery and hypnosis in the office in preparation for the live desensitization experience. This consisted of offering support as she drove, reminding her of all she learned during the office sessions. When she drove with relative ease she discovered she could apply the coping skills she had acquired to any driving experience.

One day she said she was ready to go over the Tobin Bridge in Boston, Massachusetts. This particular bridge is the largest in New England, spanning over two miles and going over the Mystic River. I thought it would be a major success for anyone with this phobia to go over this bridge. I think at the time I admired her courage for wanting to attempt it.

However, if she ran into difficulty I would not be able to drive for her because I had broken my right ankle and it was in a cast. I thought we would be ok despite my broken ankle because she was driving successfully with minimal discomfort while going on some highways and the expressway. She gave me every indication she was ready, so I said ok and across the bridge we went.

We entered the lower northbound deck in mid-morning with minimal traffic. The movement was easy going at about 25 miles an hour. This lower deck has kind of a closed-in feeling because the ceiling is the upper deck. It is only 36 ft. wide with no breakdown lane.

About half way across she had a panic attack. She started yelling she could not do it and stopped the car right there in the middle of the bridge with no place to pull over! I realized that with a broken ankle I could not drive even if we could have pulled over. What would that teach her anyway!

The only way over it was **Through It**. I was aware and concerned that we could be hit by the cars behind us, though they seemed to just go around us.

Somehow, I pulled up all my resources and talked her **Through It**. I did not stop talking until we were across the bridge and able to pull over to a parking place on one of the side streets.

Ahhhh! Taking some deep breaths we relaxed and talked about what had just happened. She was in good shape, though nervous, and we went back across to the other side. This time we were on the upper deck and had to go onto a major highway as we came off the bridge. Two birds with one stone, as the saying goes.

She was fine and well on her way to being able to cross bridges and drive the expressway without panic. A major achievement, except that because of the traumatic experience of crossing the bridge with her I developed a phobia of being a passenger in a car!

I had unresolved trauma in my own system after that experience. Whenever I was a passenger in a car I found myself grabbing the door handle, stomping on the invisible brake pedal as if to stop the car and yelling directions at the driver. This happened especially with my husband, who was at a loss about how to respond.

No matter what I did I could not get fully over this phobia. I used hypnosis, Neurolinguistic Programming, imagery, even Tapas Acupressure Technique, Emotional Freedom Technique and EMDR when those modalities became available. I could lessen the response but not fully heal it.

Last year, 25 years later, as a passenger in the back seat I had an intense phobic reaction when I was driving with some other therapists on the West Side Highway in New York City. That is when I decided that I had to do something else to clear this reaction.

I asked the question "what occurred in the first bear experience that did not occur in the car experience that led to this difficult response?" In both I was not hurt and I used my resources to help me. However, several very important things happened in the bear experience that did not happen in the driving one.

- First, I got to talk about it, share it and be believed.
- Second, I got to move right away by hiking out of the woods and into the camping area.

- Next, about 24 hours after the event, I got to fully connect with the fear, terror really and respond by running down the trail. As a result, all of the chemicals coursing through my body got metabolized and I got to fully integrate on all levels with the fullness of the experience.

I did not get to do this in the driving incident and I was left with a part of me believing that being a passenger in a car was dangerous. Since I did not get to fully connect with and process the fear my system kept taking me back to it in an attempt to process it.

Once I understood this, I went for a slow jog. I remembered that original event of being on the bridge and many of the other times I was afraid as a passenger. While I jogged I put my attention on those events, the beliefs I had about myself, the emotions and especially the fear I experienced. Continuing to jog, I went into the TAT hold or alternately tapped my upper arms. I concentrated on all those memories especially connecting to the fear. I never fully felt the same terror I had with the bear experience but that did not seem to matter. After about 20 minutes I felt done. I was more relaxed and less attached to the various fearful occurrences. Since then my reactivity in the car has significantly reduced. I can now tolerate and even enjoy being a passenger. My husband and I find ourselves singing, laughing or telling stories as we drive in commuter traffic.

Finding Ways to Clear the Blocks

"As my mind can conceive of more good, the barriers and blocks dissolve. My life becomes full of little miracles popping up out of the blue" **Louise Hay**

Sometimes these blocks are easily cleared with mindful activity including positive self-talk, or using a process like TAT, EFT, imagery, meditation and breathing. Sometimes it is necessary to seek additional help. You might need to find a therapist or counselor trained in mind/body modalities to help you clear the stress and the blocks. There are many treatment methods useful in clearing traumatic stress. I have listed a number of them below. Being connected to positive Qualities of Self will better enable you to do that processing. It is a balancing act and has to be done gently. Give yourself time to adjust to the changes that are happening within.

The Effectiveness of Tapas Acupressure Technique®

"If you really believe in what you're doing, work hard, take nothing personally and if something blocks one route, find another. Never give up." Laurie Notaro

Keep in mind that as you clear away one block it is not unusual for some others to surface. You may have to keep clearing the blocks over a few days or weeks to experience the fullness of the healing.

Tapas Acupressure Technique® (TAT®) is an effective, easy and safe tool to use for clearing many of the blocks and reactions to life's stressful events. TAT is a self-administered stabilization and relaxation process that utilizes several acupoints around the eyes and the back of the head while placing one's attention on various aspects of a problem.

Tapas Fleming, an acupuncturist, developed this technique in 1993 when she was working with allergic reactions. She wanted to find something that would clear the sensitivity to the allergen and allow the person to be non-reactive to that substance (such as eggs, milk, etc.).

One day as she was pondering this dilemma, she woke up from a nap with the idea that if she stimulated two points on the inside of the eyes it would help clear the allergy. She began to try it and then added a third point in between the eyebrows.

She found very quickly that when the patient put her/his attention on the allergen while these points were stimulated, the allergy receded. At some point during this process she added holding the back of the skull on the occipital bone, which corresponds to the vision center for the brain.

One client came in with a salt allergy and Tapas used this process. At the end of the first session, the woman said that when she was young she was repeatedly abused in a bar and after each time she was given a bag of potato chips. This was the first time she was able to remember all of those incidents in her life with no emotional stress. She had done years of "talk" therapy, which hadn't resolved the issue. After this one treatment, both the allergy to salt and the trauma related to the events disappeared.

What I find over and over again is that when a person (including myself) holds these points and puts her/his attention on a problem, the stress related to this problem eases. They can, in a matter of a few minutes, feel more stabilized.

In brain wave studies, J. Andrake, MD illustrated how stimulating certain acupoints while activating an anxiety-evoking image sent signals to the brain that neutralized the affected brain wave patterns. The electrochemical shifts that occur correspond to a reduction in the strong emotional affect felt at the time, such as a reduction in the experience of fear connected to a phobic reaction.

TAT is invaluable in my work with traumatic stress. It is a user friendly technique that you can easily integrate into your life. The full protocol includes gently touching three spots around the eyes and holding the back of the head while following a nine step process. This can be adapted to a three-part or even a one-part process. Please go to www.tatlife.com for further information and to download the booklet.

"TAT helps liberate us from identification with anything we are not, and return us to the peace of who we are."
Tapas Fleming

Experiential with TAT:

First: go to www.TATLIFE.com and download TAT for a Stressful Event. Read it over.

Next: Put your attention on a problem: Describe it here (or in your journal):

_____

_____

_____

_____

_____

_____

_____

_____

_____

Next: Pick two or three qualities you would like to connect with to help you with this problem. Write them here:

_____

_____

_____

_____

Next: Notice what comes up around the problem. What are the stopper thoughts or limiting beliefs to those qualities? Include emotions, thoughts, beliefs, experiences, sensations. Write them here:

_____

_____

_____

_____

_____

Be Resilient: Free Your Glorious Self

_____

_____

_____

_____

_____

_____

_____

_____

Then: Putting your attention on all you have written, follow the steps in the download. If you have difficulty you can always contact me or another certified TAT professional to do an individual session. Sometimes having support and guidance are important as you begin to clear these blocks.

An Example: When my son was an early teen he would do things in a way that got me upset. I was mostly able to tolerate it, get annoyed but continue on. One day he did something that really riled me. I lost my self-control. I had a temper tantrum complete with yelling and screaming.

I was no longer yelling at my son but at my brothers as a teen. All that pent up unprocessed anger came pouring out. My son ran for cover and my husband came running in wondering what was going on.

Fortunately, I calmed down and realized what was happening. I came back to my fully resourced Adult Self. Together with the help of my husband and TAT, I processed what happened to me.

I shared the memories and leftover emotions of being taunted by my brothers that came rushing in when my son spoke to me in that manner. I was able to utilize TAT to clear the leftover feelings and heal from those difficult memories, emotions and beliefs.

Once I was more fully resourced and connected to the Glorious Being within, my husband and I respectfully went into our son's room and processed it with him. I apologized, made amends and also gave him an opportunity to talk about his feelings. He did not talk a lot but allowed us all to do TAT on all the drama and trauma this experience had for him.

Not only did I get to clear one of my buried "treasures" but my son also got to have a learning experience of mending a fracture in the relationship with compassion, empathy and understanding.

And, believe it or not a few months later one of those brothers, with whom I had no contact for years, sent me a gift. Clearly someone else got the benefit of this healing.

Leftovers

The stress of life can sometimes disconnect you from those qualities that you have at your core; even the ones you spent many hours developing in your growing-up years. It is helpful to reconnect as best you can with those qualities so they can help you as you release the leftovers of difficult and traumatic experience. You already have mirror neurons and other neural networks that simply need to be remembered, reactivated and strengthened.

Here is something else you can do:

> Cross your hands over your heart and have a conversation with the blocks as if they are parts of you. Let these parts of you know you love and accept them. Let them know that all you want for them is to be fully connected to your shared

Glorious Self. Notice what comes up for you and them. Stay present with it. Write about it here:

Other Modalities:

- **Energy psychology and spiritual modalities** include Emotional Freedom Technique (EFT), Thought Field Therapy (TFT), REIKI, Qi Gong, Yoga

   The Association for Comprehensive Energy Psychology (ACEP) www.energypsych.org is a great resource for learning about different modalities useful in clearing stress and building resources.

REMAP (Reed Eye Movement Acupressure Psychotherapy) "has a central focus of calming the emotional midbrain and soothing the sympathetic nervous system in order to counter conditioned responses. Through innovative applications of acupressure, mindfulness, breath regulation and activation of regions within the visual field, REMAP works from body to brain in order to desensitize emotional distress. Through this mechanism, the REMAP methods help to retrain the limbic system to make associations of relaxation and comfort with memories that were previously coded as painful." Steve Reed http://remapinstitute.org

Eye Movement Desensitization and Reprocessing is an evidence based treatment modality for post traumatic stress disorder (PTSD), adverse life events, and somatic symptoms including pain. It has been proven successful for PTSD in 16 published controlled, randomized studies, with comparisons to antidepressant medication, cognitive behavioral therapies, and other forms of therapy.

Following an eight step process EMDR utilizes alternating bilateral and dual attention stimulation in the form of eye movements, alternate sounds or alternate tapping on the knees or shoulders to facilitate normal information processing and integration of past experience, current triggers and future challenges. It is postulated that the alternate eye movements simulate REM (rapid eye movement) believed to be important in our daily processing of life's experiences.

EMDR is a very respected and useful therapy. You will need a professional trained in this therapy model to clear blocks and traumatic stress with EMDR. It is very helpful to build up your resourcefulness so you can utilize EMDR to its fullest.

I used EMDR to help me clear the phobia of being a passenger in a car.

Mindful Meditation:

"Dedicating some time to meditation is a meaningful expression of caring for yourself that can help you move through the mire of feeling unworthy of recovery. As your mind grows quieter and more spacious, you can begin to see self-defeating thought patterns for what they are, and open up to other, more positive options" Sharon Salzberg

Meditation and Your Brain

"Meditation makes the entire nervous system go into a field of coherence" Deepak Chopra

Meditation, relaxation and mindfulness can immediately change your state of mind and also rework the very structure of your brain. Studies have shown that stimulating activity in the left pre-frontal areas of the brain bring about the experience of positive mood or a more steady positive outlook. Long-term meditation practice develops brains that both enjoy and maintain an experience of positive well-being, even at stressful times.

"What Fires Together Wires Together, What fires Apart Wires Apart" Hebb's axiom

Neuropsychologist Rick Hanson says that "Stimulating areas of the brain that handle positive emotions strengthens those neural networks, just as working muscles strengthens them."

The opposite is also true "If you routinely think about things that make you feel mad or wounded, you are sensitizing and strengthening the amygdala, which is primed to respond to negative experiences. So it will become more reactive, and you will get more upset more easily in the future. You can use your mind to change your brain to affect your mind."

If you routinely spend time in meditative practices it can have an overall positive effect on your brain, your body and your life. Here are just some of the overall effects of mindful meditation:

- sense of overall well being
- improved internal awareness of your body
- building an improved pleasant sense of being in your body
- greater sensitivity to "gut feelings" and intuition
- increased empathy for others
- increased ability to tolerate and not get so distraught with anger, fear, shame, and sorrow.

Here are some easy to do mindful meditation practices:

Kirtan Kriya is a type of meditation that brings together repetitive chanting with finger movements.

The chanting uses the sounds of Saa, Taa, Naa, and Maa. First saying them out loud, then whispering them, then repeating the sounds silently, and finally reversing the sequence. Each sound also has a corresponding finger movement (e.g. thumb touches pointer finger). This entire meditation sequence is done in 12 minutes but can be extended to 15, 18 or 21 minutes.

A small pilot study using Kirtan Kriya meditation to improve memory was published in 2010 in *Journal of Alzheimer's Disease*. Fifteen people (ages 52-77) with memory loss practiced Kirtan Kriya for 12 minutes a day for eight weeks. They had a small control group who listened to Mozart violin concertos for the same amount of time.

The meditation group showed improved cerebral blood flow, statistically significant improvements in a neuropsychological test measuring cognition, and improvements in three other cognitive tests that measured general memory, attention and cognition.

Try it, You'll like it

Direction: Kirtan Kriya 12 minute meditation:

Breathe deeply before and after

Chant or say out loud for two minutes:
Chant **saa** while touching thumb to pointer finger (corresponds to wisdom)
Chant **taa** while touching thumb to middle finger (corresponds to discipline)
Chant **naa** while touching thumb to fourth (ring) finger (corresponds to light)

Chant **maa** while touching thumb to little finger (corresponds to communication)

Whisper for two minutes
Whisper **saa** while touching thumb to pointer finger
Whisper **taa** while touching thumb to middle finger
Whisper **naa** while touching thumb to ring finger
Whisper **maa** while touching thumb to little finger

Silently for two minutes
Say silently **saa** while touching thumb to pointer finger
Say silently **taa** while touching thumb to middle finger
Say silently **naa** while touching thumb to ring finger
Say silently **maa** while touching thumb to little finger

Repeat. Begin with silent for two minutes, then Whisper for two minutes, then out loud for two minutes, Breathe deeply and stretch arms overhead

YOU TUBE Videos demonstrating Kirtan Kriya

http://bit.ly/1BgXwwS

http://bit.ly/1utAww2

Breathing

"The sun, the earth, love, friends, our very breath are parts of the banquet." Rebecca Harding Davis

6 Breaths per minute: This particular breathing technique has been shown to quickly reduce the heart rate. Even a few minutes can reduce mild to moderate anxiety

- Inhale and exhale for five seconds each
- Inhale Count "in, 2, 3, 4, 5"
- Exhale "out, 2, 3, 4, 5
- Repeat six times for a total of 60 seconds
- Then continue for as long as you choose

"I took a deep breath and listened to the old bray of my heart. I am. I am. I am" Sylvia Plath

Metta (Loving kindness) Meditation: Another easy to use meditation which you can do anywhere, riding on a bus or a train or in a car, walking, in bed. I find it especially helpful when I am having difficulty sleeping.

Sit comfortably, relax, be at ease, cross your hands over your chest and repeat the following statements over and over again.

May I be safe and protected
May I be well
May I be peaceful
May I be fully at ease

Then think about someone close to you, imagine them and direct loving kindness to them

May you be safe and protected
May you be well
May you be peaceful
May you be fully at ease

Then think about someone who you are having difficulty with or holding a resentment toward. Imagine them in front of you and direct loving kindness to them

May you be safe and protected
May you be well
May you be peaceful
May you be fully at ease

Be Resilient: Free Your Glorious Self

Then think about the wider community, even the world, imagine them and direct loving kindness to them

> May you be safe and protected
> May you be well
> May you be peaceful
> May you be fully at ease

Here are a couple of You Tube demonstrations of Loving Kindness Meditation

http://www.youtube.com/watch?v=W3uLqt69VyI

http://bit.ly/1xpG1Ni

"At the end of the day, I can end up just totally wacky, because I've made mountains out of molehills. With meditation, I can keep them as molehills." Ringo Starr

Be Resilient: Free Your Glorious Self

Chapter 5: Fully Integrate These Qualities Into Your Life

"Practice Makes Progress" **-** David Roth, Musician

Listen here: http://www.youtube.com/watch?v=ybFBprnUXQ8

Put your attention back on the Positive Quality or Qualities you chose back in Chapter 3. What happens now?

Cross your hands over your heart and invite that quality or qualities to come fully in...see it... feel it... hear it... taste it... smell it...

Be Resilient: Free Your Glorious Self

After you spend some time doing this then write about that here:

_____

_____

_____

_____

_____

_____

_____

_____

_____

_____

_____

_____

Be Resilient: Free Your Glorious Self

Do a drawing of yourself with this quality (qualities) here or make a collage with magazine pictures, string, ribbon, and anything that grabs your fancy. This is for you, to help you more fully connect with your Glorious Being and all the wonderful positive qualities you possess.

Be Resilient: Free Your Glorious Self

As you look at this drawing put your attention on all you have done to come to this place and feel fully connected to this positive quality (qualities).

Cross your hands over your heart and repeat this message (feel free to change the words in any way that makes sense for you)

"I am grateful for all of this learning and information and I bring all of this fully into my heart now."

In the days and weeks that follow stay connected to yourself and present to your Glorious Being Within, Your Glorious Self. Be aware of what happens. Notice when you begin to go into the ruts. What beliefs are you telling yourself? How are you feeling? Keeping a journal can be helpful here.

Continue the process as you want and need. Pick a quality a day. Even if you do not do all the steps sometimes just being mindful of the desire to bring that quality more fully into your life is helpful. You learn by observing and doing. So observe those qualities in others and in yourself. Notice how you feel, act, and think when connected to those positive qualities.

Feel free to do the whole process especially when you have a Self Esteem Crash. You know, when your belief in yourself takes a dive. Something usually happens to trigger those little hurt, disconnected parts in some way and they get activated. They are there to let you know "Hey, pay attention to me, help me." Like when I had anxiety as a passenger in a car. That was just my little-self saying "I'm here, please help me." When I did she could integrate fully and we could all enjoy the ride!

You too can connect with and integrate all of the qualities you need to live your life from your most Resourced, Glorious Self

"If you make up your mind to be happy no one and nothing can take that happiness from you."

  P. Yogananda

In Closing

Please take advantage of offerings at the website www.thelifeworkscenter.com

There is a free download with a list of qualities with quotes and suggestions which you can use as a daily practice. **http://bit.ly/1qyNNMd**

There are webinars, in person workshops, individual consultation available to help you in your quest to Free your Glorious Self!

Please feel free to contact me with any questions, responses or requests at patthatch@thelifeworkscenter.com

I wish you many blessings as you continue on your journey to fully connecting with and living from Your Glorious Self!

"You may encounter many defeats,
but you must not be defeated.
In fact, it may be necessary to encounter the defeats,
so you can know who you are,
what you can rise from,
how you can still come out of it."

Maya Angelou ~

Be Resilient: Free Your Glorious Self

Chapter 6: Qualities and Characteristics

Here is a list of qualities you can use while you do the exercises. Please feel free to add to this list if any come to mind that are not mentioned.

These definitions are taken from Encarta North America online dictionary, Miriam Webster online Dictionary and Bing.

**based on the work of Shirley Jean Schmidt, DNMS (developmental needs meets strategy) www.shirleyjeanschmidt.com

Accepting: to take or receive (something offered); receive with approval or favor. Willing to acknowledge and tolerate without trying to change. Able to endure something difficult or unpleasant without complaint or protest.

Accepting of Others **: Willing to acknowledge and tolerate without trying to change. Willingness to treat somebody as a member of a group or social circle.

Action-Taker**: Able to do something in order to achieve a purpose.

Alert: watchful and ready to deal with whatever happens; clear-headed and responsive

Appropriately Responsible**: Being accountable to somebody for an action or for the successful carrying out of a duty. Able to be counted on owing to qualities of conscientiousness and trustworthiness. Not taking on more responsibility than is appropriate.

Attunement: Able to adjust or accustom something to be receptive or responsive to something else.

Balance: a state of emotional and mental stability in which somebody is calm and able to make rational decisions and judgments.

Be Resilient: Free Your Glorious Self

Belonging: the state of being accepted and comfortable in a place or group.

Bold: willing and eager to face danger or adventure with a sense of confidence and fearlessness.

Caring: compassionate or showing concern for others and self.

Centered: Exhibiting confidence, self-awareness, and often a sense of determination.

Clarity: clearness of expression: the quality of being clearly expressed; clearness of thought: clearness in what somebody is thinking.

Compassion: showing feelings of sympathy for the suffering of others, often with a desire to help.

Competent: having enough skill or ability to do something well

Confidence: self-assurance or a belief in your ability to succeed. Belief or trust in somebody or something, or in the ability of somebody or something to act in a proper, trustworthy, or reliable manner

Courageous: Able to face danger, difficulty, uncertainty, or pain without being overcome by fear or being deflected from a chosen course of action.

Creativity: the ability to use the imagination to develop new and original ideas or things, especially in an artistic context.

Curious: eager to know about something or to get information.

Decision-Maker**: Able to make choices or reach conclusions, especially on important matters.

Dedicated: wholeheartedly devoted or committed to a goal, cause, or job.

Detachment: lack of involvement; objectivity; a lack of bias, prejudice, or emotional involvement.

Empathy: the ability to identify with and understand somebody else's feelings or difficulties.

Empowered: to possess a greater sense of confidence or self-esteem; one who possesses power or authority.

Be Resilient: Free Your Glorious Self

Enthusiasm: lively interest

Faith: allegiance or loyalty to somebody or something.

Firm: fixed securely and unlikely to give way; showing certainty or determination.

Gentleness: having a mild and kind nature or manner; being moderate in force or degree so that the effects are not severe.

Good At Listening**: Able to pay attention to something and take it into account.

Graceful: marked by poise, dignity, and politeness.

Grounded: Having a secure feeling of being in touch with reality and personal feelings.

Hope: to have a wish to get or do something or for something to happen or be true, especially something that seems possible or likely.

Humorous: witty or able to make people laugh.

Integrated: combined or composite; made up of aspects or parts that work well together.

Integrity: quality of possessing and steadfastly adhering to high moral principles or professional standards

Joyful: feelings of great happiness or pleasure, especially of an elevated or spiritual kind.

Kind: having a generous warm compassionate nature; not harsh, unpleasant, or likely to have destructive effects; showing generosity or compassion

Laughter: to make sounds from the throat while breathing out in short bursts or gasps as a way of expressing amusement

Letting Go: to allow or cause something to pass from one place to another. To stop holding something.

Lightness: total freedom from worry and trouble.

Logical: Able to think sensibly and come to a rational conclusion based on facts rather than emotion.

Be Resilient: Free Your Glorious Self

Nurturing: to give tender care and protection to a young child, animal, or plant, helping it to grow and develop; to keep a feeling in the mind for a long time, allowing it to grow or deepen

Open: Ready and willing to accept or listen to something such as new ideas or suggestions. Very free or generous. The state of being no longer hidden or held back.

Patient: Able to endure waiting, delay, or provocation without becoming annoyed or upset. Able to persevere calmly, especially when faced with difficulties.

Peace: freedom from conflict or disagreement among people or groups of people.

Perseverance: steady and continued action or belief, usually over a long period and especially despite difficulties or setbacks.

Playfulness: the state of being fond of having fun and playing games with others.

Presence: ability to stay present and mindful of what is occurring in the moment

Problem-Solver**: Able to find a way of dealing successfully with a problem or difficulty.

Protective: Preventing somebody or something from being harmed or damaged, or designed or intended for this purpose.

Reliable: Able to be trusted to do what is expected or has been promised.

Resilience: The ability to recover quickly from setbacks. The ability of matter to spring back into shape after being bent, stretched or deformed.

Respectful: showing appropriate deference and respect (a feeling or attitude of admiration and deference toward somebody or something). Able to be courteous.

Safe: in a position or situation that offers protection, so that harm, damage, loss, or unwanted tampering is unlikely.

Satisfaction: The feeling of pleasure that comes when a need or desire is fulfilled; happiness with the way that something has been arranged or done.

Self-acceptance: Willing to acknowledge and tolerate without trying to change it

Self-esteem: to have a high regard, opinion and appreciation for self. Holding self as being worthwhile.

Self-love: to feel tender affection for self with an attitude of respect

Setting appropriate Boundaries: Setting limits on behavior of self and others in order to create safety and comfort.

Spiritual: relating to the soul or spirit, usually in contrast to material things.

Stable: having a calm and steady temperament, rather than being excitable or given to apparently irrational behavior.

Strong: Having the necessary emotional qualities to deal with stress, grief, loss, risk, and other difficulties; being in good health.

Supportive: to give active help, encouragement, or money to somebody or something; to give assistance or comfort to somebody in difficulty or distress.

Tolerance: the acceptance of the differing views of other people; the act of putting up with somebody or something irritating or otherwise unpleasant

Tranquility: a state of peace and calm.

Trustworthy: Deserving trust, or able to be trusted. Dependable.

Understanding: The ability to perceive and explain the meaning or the nature of somebody or something; a sympathetic, empathetic, or tolerant recognition of somebody else's nature or situation.

Warm: affectionate, kind, friendly.

Wise: able to make sensible decisions and judgments on the basis of personal knowledge and experience; showing good sense or good judgment.

Be Resilient: Free Your Glorious Self

GLORIOUS BEING WITHIN

WISE SELF

Accepting
Present
Compassionate
Safe
Curious
Playful
CHILD
Connected
Loving
Clear
Understanding

Graphic by Beth Rontal, LICSW

Chapter 7: References

Ruth M. Buczynski, PhD The National Institute for the Clinical Application of Behavioral Medicine http://www.nicabm.com

Benson, Herbert, MD and Proctor, William (2011) *Relaxation Revolution: The Science and Genetics of Mind Body Healing* Simon and Shuster, NY

Church, Pamela V. (2007) *Gestures of the Heart: A Guide for Healing the Residue of Life's Trauma's.* Pamela V. Church, Amazon.com

Diamond, John, MD. (1979) *Your Body Doesn't Lie.* New York: Warner books

Doidge, Norman MD. (2007) *The Brain that Changes Itself.* New York: Penguin

Dossey, L. (1993) H*ealing Words: The power of prayer and the practice of medicine.* San Francisco: Harper

Elder, Charles MD, MPH et al. "Randomized Trial of two mind-body interventions for weight loss management" *Journal of Alternative and Complimentary Medicine*, Vol 13, Number 1, 2007, pg 67-78

Erickson, Milton, M.D., Rossi, Ernest L. (1989) *The February Man.* Bruner Mazel

Fleming, Tapas, L.Ac. (2011) *TAT Professionals' Manual,* Redondo Beach, Ca: TAT International, web site www.tatlife.com phone 877-828-4685

Hanson, Rick (2009) *Buddha's Brain: The Practical Neuroscience of Happiness, Love, and Wisdom*, New Harbinger

Herman, Judith Lewis, M.D. (1992) *Trauma and Recovery* New York: Basic Books

Iacoboni, Marco MD, PhD, (2008) *Mirroring People:* The Science of Empathy and How We Connect with Others , Farrar, Straus and Giroux, NY

Korn, D.L., & Leeds, A.M. (2002) "Preliminary evidence of efficacy for EMDR resource development and installation in the stabilization phase of treatment of complex posttraumatic stress disorder" *Journal of Clinical Psychology*, 58(12), 1465-1487

Lipton, Bruce, M.D.(2008) *The Biology of Belief* Hay House

Levine, Peter A. (1997) *Waking The Tiger: Healing Trauma.* North Atlantic Books

Pert, Candace, PhD. (1997) *Molecules of Emotion.* New York: Simon & Shuster

Seels, B. & Glasgow, Z. (1997). *Making Instructional Design Decisions*, 2nd ed. Upper Saddle River, NJ: Prentice Hall, 1997.

Shapiro, F. (2012) *Getting Past Your Past: Take Control of Your Life with Self-Help Techniques from EMDR Therapy.* Rodale

Siegel, DJ & Bryson, TP. (2012) *The Whole-Brain Child: 12 Revolutionary Strategies to Nurture Your Child's Developing Mind.* New York: Bantam

van der Kolk, Bessel, M.D (2014)*The Body Keeps the Score: Brain, Mind, and Body in the Healing of Trauma.* Amazon

Testimonials:

"This book not only teaches you how to immediately access inner resources you might not have even known you had, you actually feel uplifted and more in touch with what's possible for you just from reading the book! The exercises Pat gives are simple, powerful and effective. I know -- I tried one out and it worked for me!"
Tapas Fleming, Creator of Tapas Acupressure Technique®

Knowing your work as well as I do after these years of trainings and supervision I am so happy to hear your warm, down to earth and encouraging voice describe the path to healing so clearly. This book is a very client and therapist friendly resource. I appreciate its brevity and accessibility for those who struggle with the effects of trauma. There is a fine balance of brain science and practical suggestions. Your ideas for developing inner and outer resources are essential for anyone seeking to feel safe and healed. I will definitely be suggesting this book to my clients! I hope it comes out soon.
Elissa Pearmain, LMHC

"What I like about it is that it is a simple, positive, straightforward way toward being a positive person. I find myself looking forward to doing the exercises and feeling a feeling of being positive, of hopefulness as I read."
Katherine Reeder, LMHC

I've been an expert in the field of self help for over 20 years, yet the book *Be Resilient: Free Your Glorious Self* opened my eyes to some new techniques. I used the simple straight forward instructions to dissolve an old wound in seconds and I will definitely use this book with my clients.
Jasmine White, The Healing Business Coach

Be Resilient: Free Your Glorious Self

Be Resilient: Free Your Glorious Self